FOOD BRANDS WE LOVE

HERSHEY

By Kaitlyn Duling

Kaleidoscope
Minneapolis, MN

The Quest for Discovery Never Ends

This edition is co-published by agreement between Kaleidoscope and World Book, Inc.

Kaleidoscope Publishing, Inc.
6012 Blue Circle Drive
Minnetonka, MN 55343 U.S.A.

World Book, Inc.
180 North LaSalle St., Suite 900
Chicago IL 60601 U.S.A.

Kaleidoscope ISBNs
978-1-64519-211-4 (library bound)
978-1-64519-279-4 (ebook)

World Book ISBN
978-0-7166-4189-6 (library bound)

Library of Congress Control Number
2020936230

Developed and produced by Focus Strategic Communications Inc.

Printed in the United States of America.

FIND ME IF YOU CAN!

Bigfoot lurks within one of the images in this book. It's up to you to find him!

TABLE OF CONTENTS

Chapter 1
The Sweetest Story

Dara shivered. She pulled her jacket tightly around her body. It was a cold night, but at least her mom had made a big campfire. The flames crackled and danced. Dara, her parents, and her brothers had just finished roasting hot dogs. It was fun…until Dara's hot dog fell in the dirt. Her stomach grumbled. "What a klutz, dropping your food," Dara's brother teased, "Lucky for you, it's time for s'mores." Dara rolled her eyes. Her stomach grumbled even louder. S'mores would do the trick. She grabbed a puffy marshmallow and found a sharp stick. Time to roast.

FUN FACT

The first Hershey's bars cost just two cents (2¢).

The first step in making a s'more is roasting a marshmallow.

S'mores consist of marshmallows and chocolate between two graham crackers.

With a paper plate balanced on her knees, Dara built her s'more. She laid out two graham cracker squares. Then she opened the crinkly wrapper of a Hershey's bar. "Mmm," she said, "The chocolate is the best part." Carefully, Dara placed one toasted marshmallow on top of the chocolate. Not too melted.

It was just right. She squished a graham cracker on top. Done. A s'more was the perfect treat. It tasted even better than she imagined. She didn't drop as much as a crumb on the ground.

A Hershey kiss is a small, bite-sized chocolate candy shaped like a teardrop.

FUN FACT

When Hershey's Kisses were introduced, they were wrapped by hand.

Hershey is the largest chocolate manufacturer in North America.

Halloween is an important date for Hershey chocolate candy.

Hershey's bars are an important **ingredient** in s'mores. No campfire is complete without them. Similarly, Hershey's candies have become a key part of countless celebrations and special events. People eat Hershey's chocolate on Valentine's Day, Christmas, and Halloween. All over the globe, children and adults share the joy of biting into sweet, silky Hershey's bars. The **brand** is beloved for its delicious treats and long history. From big cities to small towns, in offices and classrooms, people like Dara bite into Hershey's bars. They also munch on Hershey's Kisses, Krackel, Mr. Goodbar, and many other candies. Yum!

Chapter 2
History of Hershey

The Hershey's story is over 100 years old. The brand was started by a man named Milton Hershey. Chocolate from faraway countries like France and Switzerland is prized for its rich taste. But you don't have to go far to visit the home of Milton Hershey. He started his company in Pennsylvania.

Have you ever heard of the Lancaster Caramel Company? Probably not. That was Milton Hershey's first successful business. In the late 1890s, he sold the company for $1 million ($30 million in today's dollars). He wanted to shift his focus to chocolate bars.

FUN FACT
The very first Hershey's product was Hershey's Cocoa. It was introduced in 1894.

DON'T STOP BELIEVIN'

Milton Hershey had a rocky path to success. He didn't graduate high school. Instead, he became an apprentice to a candy maker. He started two businesses—and failed at both. Hershey didn't start his chocolate company until he reached his 30s. He became known as The Chocolate King.

"Welcome to Hershey" is spelled out in white stones on the lawn of Hotel Hershey.

In 1903, Hershey construction crews began working night and day. They were building the world's largest chocolate factory. Why was it so big? Because, after years of trying, Hershey had finally perfected his recipe. Once the public tasted Hershey's chocolate, it was love at first bite.

Milton Hershey didn't stop there. Around the factory, he built an entire town. It had schools and houses. Hershey paid for it all with the profits from his candy. The popularity of Hershey's products continued to grow. Candy fans couldn't get enough.

Today, the town of Hershey is home to an amusement park, a zoo, and a Hershey museum. It's a popular spot for **tourists**. Though Milton Hershey passed away in 1945, his brand lives on. Hershey employs over 16,000 workers. In 2019, it had $7.8 billion in sales. That's a lot of chocolate.

Hershey's Chocolate World in Hershey, PA, was the first of five locations. The others include Times Square in New York City, Las Vegas, Niagara Falls, and Singapore.

HERSHEY'S

TIMELINE

1857
Milton Snavely Hershey is born in Hockersville, Pennsylvania.

1893
At the World's Columbian Exposition in Chicago, Milton Hershey purchases chocolate-making equipment.

1894
Hershey's Cocoa is introduced.

1900
Hershey sells the Lancaster Caramel Company for $1 million.

1903
Hershey begins to build a chocolate-making factory in Pennsylvania.

1906
Hersheypark is built.

1907
Hershey's Kisses are introduced.

1909
The Milton Hershey School opens.

1857 1893 1894 1900 1903 1907 1909

1938
Krackel candy bars are introduced.

1973
The first Hershey's Chocolate World opens in Hershey, PA.

1918
Hershey gives most of his fortune to the M.S. Hershey Foundation.

1989
Hershey's Symphony bars are introduced.

1918 1926 1938 1970 1973 1989 1994

1970
Hershey creates its first **advertisements**.

1926
Hershey's Syrup is introduced.

1994
Hershey's Cookies 'n' Creme Bar is introduced.

Chapter 3

Doing Good

Cole's eyes traced the lines of the tall roller coaster. His neck tilted back. He spotted the steep drop. "Gulp." Coasters were fun, but they made him nervous. Cole had never ridden this one before. It was a new coaster at Hersheypark.

Everything at Hersheypark was fun. There was endless candy and thrilling rides. Cole was surprised. He hadn't been excited about the family vacation. But yesterday, his family visited the Hershey Story Museum. They learned all about the history of the park. That made the story come alive.

The Hershey Story is the company museum located on Chocolate Avenue in Hershey, PA.

The Lightning Racer is one of 13 roller coasters in Hersheypark.

The Hershey Trolley Works takes tourists on a 45-minute tour of Hershey's Chocolate World.

The park was built in the early 1900s. Why? Because Milton Hershey wanted his workers to have fun. He knew it was important to take breaks from work. Hershey also built a trolley system and houses. He even built a zoo.

ZooAmerica in Hersheypark features animals form North America.

Cole learned that the company had always been focused on **philanthropy**. In 1909, Milton Hershey started a school for orphans. Today, the Milton Hershey School is a boarding school for children in need. It is located on the Hershey homestead, the house where Milton was born.

FUN FACT

In 2018, Hershey donated $8 million to nonprofits. They also donated 133,000 employee volunteer hours, and $10.5 million worth of products.

Milton Hershey founded a school for orphans in 1909.

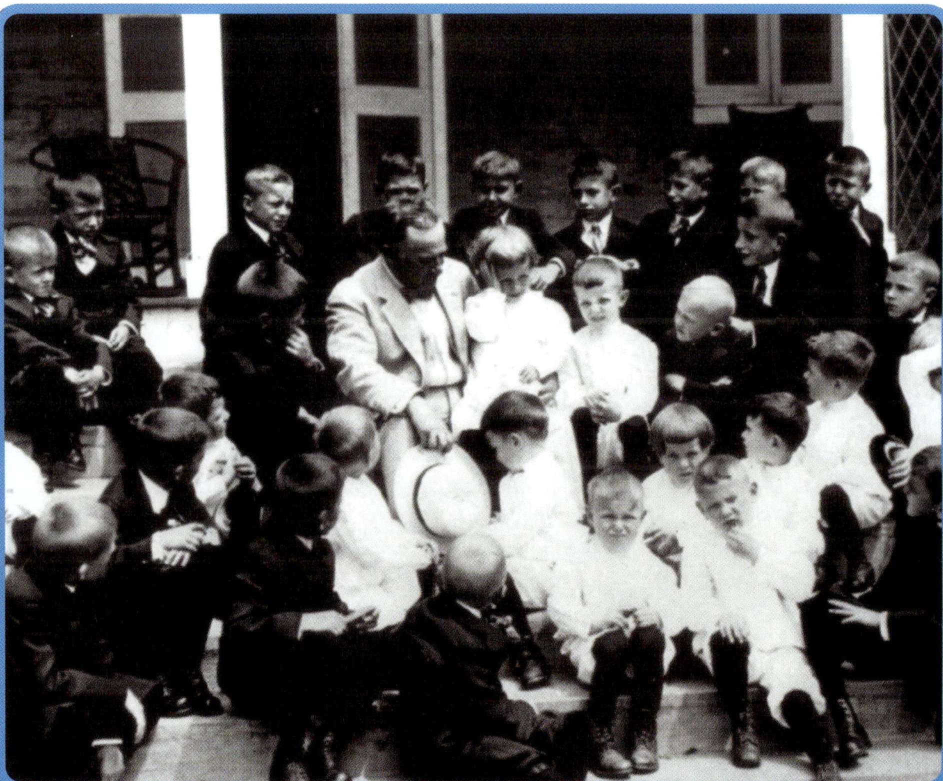

The Storm Rider roller coaster plunges from zero to 72 mph in just two seconds.

While he waited in line for the coaster, Cole remembered all of the interesting things he had learned at the museum. He knew that Hershey made chocolate. But it was clear that the company also made a difference. Suddenly, Cole was at the front of the line. It was now or never. He sat down in the coaster car, closed his eyes, and held on tight.

BUILDING HERSHEY

The 1930s were marked by the **Great Depression**. Workers across the country and around the world lost their jobs. But Milton Hershey started the Great Building Campaign. He put over 600 men to work on projects around the town. The Hotel Hershey at Hersheypark first opened in 1933.

Chapter 4
More Than a Chocolate Bar

Sarah sprinted into the house. She plopped down on the living room floor. The long tail of her dragon costume stuck out behind her. Sarah turned her plastic pumpkin-shaped bucket upside-down. Hundreds of candies spilled onto the carpet. Jackpot!

Trick-or-treating was fun, but Sarah's favorite part came afterward. She loved to sort the candy. She pushed all of the Hershey bars into one pile. Cookies 'n' Creme had its own pile. Reese's had its own area. Whoppers and Almond Joys were set aside to give to her dad. He liked those.

FUN FACT

The factory in Hershey, Pennsylvania, produces more than 60 million Hershey's Kisses a day.

Halloween and Hershey were made for each other.

Hershey's Miniatures and Kisses are popular Halloween treats.

HERSHEY'S CANDY

CHOCOLATE

Hershey's
Hershey's Kisses
Reese's
Kit Kat
Almond Joy
Mounds
Heath
Mr. Goodbar
Whoppers
Whatchamacallit
Symphony
York
Cadbury
5th Avenue
Brookside

NUTS & CARAMEL

Cadbury
Milk Duds
PayDay
Rolo
Zagnut
Zero

MINTS & GUM

Ice Breakers
Breath Savers
Bubble Yum

OTHER

Jolly Rancher
Twizzlers
Good & Plenty

Sarah moved on to the non-chocolate candies. Good & Plenty, Jolly Rancher, and Twizzlers all went into the same pile. Bubble Yum and Ice Breakers were grouped together. That's when Sarah's mom walked by. "Wow!" she exclaimed, "you've got quite the Hershey's haul tonight." Sarah raised her eyebrows, confused. "Hershey's? Mom, these are all different candies. There are just two Hershey's chocolate bars." Mom shook her head and pointed to each treat. She explained that most of the candies Sarah had sorted were made by Hershey. Only a few, like M&M's, were not.

Hershey's Kissmobile was launched in 1997. Since then, it has traveled over 250,000 miles.

Hershey started out with cocoa and chocolate bars. However, the company now makes a variety of candies, mints, and other sweets. Over the years, Hershey has **expanded**. The brand has moved into other countries, too.

Of course, Hershey will always be known for its original chocolate bar. It has been over a hundred years since Milton Hershey first started tinkering with chocolate. But his candy bar has grown into an American **icon**. What could be sweeter than that?

MEAT ON THE MENU

In 2015, Hershey branched out. The company purchased KRAVE, a beef jerky brand. Why? People were buying less candy. Salty snacks were becoming more popular in the US. Will chocolate-dipped jerky be next? Time will tell.

BEYOND THE BOOK

After reading the book, it's time to think about what you learned. Try the following exercises to jumpstart your ideas.

THINK

THAT'S NEWS TO ME. Hershey is always introducing new products, flavors, and ideas. Consider how you learn about new foods and brands. What information can be found in news articles? What about news programs on TV? Where can you go to find news you can trust?

CREATE

PRIMARY SOURCES. Primary sources provide firsthand accounts of an event. Interviews, videos, and photographs are all examples of primary sources. Create a list of the kinds of primary sources you might be able to find about Hershey.

SHARE

WHAT'S YOUR OPINION? The text states that the Hershey Company makes a difference. Do you agree with that statement? Provide evidence from the text to support your opinion. Share your position and evidence with a friend. Does your friend find the argument convincing?

GROW

DRAWING CONNECTIONS. Create a diagram that shows and explains connections between the Hershey company and the town of Hershey, Pennsylvania. How does learning about the history help you better understand Hershey?

RESEARCH NINJA

Visit *www.ninjaresearcher.com/2114* to learn how to take your research skills and book report writing to the next level.

RESEARCH

DIGITAL LITERACY TOOLS

SEARCH LIKE A PRO
Learn how to use search engines to find useful websites.

FACT OR FAKE?
Discover how you can tell a trusted website from an untrustworthy resource.

TEXT DETECTIVE
Explore how to zero in on the information you need most.

SHOW YOUR WORK
Research responsibly—learn how to cite sources.

WRITE

GET TO THE POINT
Learn how to express your main ideas.

PLAN OF ATTACK
Learn prewriting exercises and create an outline.

DOWNLOADABLE REPORT FORMS

Further Resources

BOOKS

Grack, Rachel. *Cocoa Bean to Chocolate*. Hopkins, MN: Bellwether Media, 2020.

Green, Sara. *Hershey's*. Hopkins, MN: Bellwether Media, 2015.

Heinrichs, Ann. *Pennsylvania*. North Mankato, MN: The Child's World, 2018

Leigh, Anna. *30-Minute Edible Science Projects*. Minneapolis, MN: Lerner Publishing Group, 2019.

WEBSITES

FACTSURFER

Factsurfer.com gives you a safe, fun way to find more information.

1. Go to www.factsurfer.com.
2. Enter "Hershey" into the search box and click
3. Select your book cover to see a list of related websites.

Glossary

advertisements: Public announcement or notice of a product or service.

apprentice: A person who learns a skill from an employer.

brand: The name of a product made by a company.

expanded: Became larger or more far-reaching.

Great Depression: A time of severe worldwide poverty in the 1930s.

icon: An important image or symbol that represents something.

ingredient: Elements that are combined to make a food or dish.

philanthropy: Donation of money or other gifts to good causes.

tourists: People who are traveling or visiting a certain place.

Index

PHOTO CREDITS

The images in this book are reproduced through the courtesy of: Jennifer Wallace/Shutterstock Images, front cover (Reese's); Nor Gal/Shutterstock Images, front cover (Hershey's syrup); skodonnell/iStockphoto, front cover (Hershey's Kiss, Hershey's bar), pp. 1, 7 (top), 12 (bottom), 31; foxaon1987/Shutterstock Images, p. 1 (background); Sheila Fitzgerald/Shutterstock Images, pp. 3, 25 (Good & Plenty); Keith Homan/Shutterstock Images, pp. 4, 10 (center right), 15 (top left), 25 (Jolly Rancher), 27 (Krave Beef Jerky); Jessica Ruscello/Shutterstock Images, pp. 4-5; Mark Krapels/Shutterstock Images, p. 6; Peter Simins/Pix/Michael Ochs Archives/Getty Images, p. 7 (bottom); Julie Clopper/Shutterstock Images, pp. 8-9 (top); Leena Robinson/Shutterstock Images, pp. 8-9 (bottom); National Association of State Dairy and Food Departments. *Journal of Proceedings of the Annual Convention*. 1897. 35. Web 6 May 2020, p. 10 (bottom left); Bettmann/Getty Images, p. 11; SEASTOCK/iStockphoto, p. 12 (top); Joseph Skompski/Shutterstock Images, p. 13 (top); George Sheldon/Shutterstock Images, pp. 13 (bottom), 16, 17, 18 (bottom), 22; James R. Martin/Shutterstock Images, pp. 14, 26 (bottom); Alizada Studios/Shutterstock Images, p. 15 (top right); Vikendu/Shutterstock Images, p. 15 (bottom left); Fitria Ramli/Shutterstock Images, p. 15 (bottom right); LEE SNIDER PHOTO IMAGES/Shutterstock Images, p. 18 (top); AP Images, p. 19; Carolyn Kaster/AP Images, p. 20; Leonard Mccombe/The LIFE Images Collection/Getty Images, p. 21; Phichat Phruksarojanakun/Shutterstock Images, p. 23 (top); Chris O'Meara/AP Images, p. 23 (bottom); dcwcreations/Shutterstock Images, p. 24 (Milk Duds); digitalreflections/Shutterstock Images, p. 24 (Ice Breakers); DenisMArt/Shutterstock Images, p. 24 (KitKat); mikeledray/Shutterstock Images, p. 24 (Reese's); Dave Nelson/Shutterstock Images, pp. 24, 25 (Twizzlers); Delmas Lehman/Shutterstock Images, p. 26 (top); Hong Vo/Shutterstock Images, p. 27 (beef jerky).

About the Author

Kaitlyn Duling eats chocolate every single day. She has written over 100 books for children. She lives in Washington, DC.